T0368420

COOL STUFF

A
COLLECTION
OF FAVORITE QUOTES,
ESSAYS, AND
SHORT STORIES

By Donna L. K. Chiacchia

WestBow Press books may be ordered through booksellers or by contacting:

WestBow Press
A Division of Thomas Nelson & Zondervan
1663 Liberty Drive
Bloomington, IN 47403
www.westbowpress.com
844-714-3454

ISBN: 979-8-3850-0584-0 (sc)
ISBN: 979-8-3850-0585-7 (e)

Library of Congress Control Number: 2023916131

Print information available on the last page.

WestBow Press rev. date: 9/7/2023

WESTBOW
PRESS®
A DIVISION OF THOMAS NELSON
& ZONDERVAN

How Do You Get To "Cool"?

It was a matter of discipline. I had thought about putting this book together for a long time. I thought it would be a nice little gift for special occasions.

So, I got started on it. Then, I realized that I had all these graduations and other things that required gifts and I had limited funds. I believed that giving this was better than money.

It was important that a glimpse of my soul be exposed for all to share; after all, what more would I have to offer?

While I was busy formatting this book, my Mom called to tell me that my cousin Deborah had passed away. I didn't stop creating and formatting this book; I just kept going as though nothing had happened.

I realize now that this was probably the best therapy I could have had as I accepted and made telephone call after telephone call. I just kept going until I had finished the book and made twelve copies.

I think Debbie would have liked this book. I dedicate it to her life and how she wanted to live it. She did the best she could and I will always love her with all my heart.

—Donna L. K. Chiacchia

ADDITIONAL
DEDICATIONS

To my beautiful friends, the Hunters,
whom I will always love and cherish,
no matter what!

Babsy: You always make me look good.

Barbara: You are my help and support.

Bonnie: You are my birthday buddy.

Catherine: You are my heart.

Heidi: You have stood with me before God.

Joyce: You listen to me when no one else will.

Kathy: You are the reason I excel.

Margot: You are the elegance I strive to be.

Michele: You are why "Cool Stuff" is important.

Nancy: You see my soul and protect me.

I look forward to us "hunting" now
and for all eternity.

Cool Stuff Contents

TURN YOUR FACE TO THE SUN, AND
SHADOWS FOLLOW BEHIND YOU.
—MAORI PROVERB

For the Bible
(and other great books)

Tells Me So...

Jesus said to them,
"A prophet is not without honor except in his own town,
among his relatives and in his own home."
—Mark 6:4 - NIV

Matthew 2:1-2-NIV

Now when Jesus was born in Bethlehem of Judea in the days of Herod the king, behold, there came wise men from the east to Jerusalem saying, "Where is He that is born King of the Jews? For we have seen His Star in the East, and have come to worship Him".

Jeremiah 29:11-NIV

"For I know the plans I have for you", says the Lord."Plans for good and not for evil, to give you a future and a hope."

A Woman

This is written in the Hebrew Talmud, the book where all of the sayings and preaching of Rabbis are conserved over time.

It says:

"Be very careful if you make a woman cry, because God counts her tears. The woman came out of a man's rib. Not from his feet to be walked on. Not from his head to be superior, but from the side to be equal; under the arm to be protected and next to the heart to be loved."

THE LORD BLESS YOU AND KEEP YOU;
THE LORD MAKE HIS FACE SHINE ON YOU
AND BE GRACIOUS TO YOU;
THE LORD TURN HIS FACE TOWARD YOU
AND GIVE YOU PEACE.—NUMBERS 6:24-26 - NIV

The Talmud
We do not see things as they are.
We see them as we are.
Every blade of grass has an angel
that bends over it and whispers,
"Grow! Grow!"

Billy Graham
"I've read the last page of the Bible. It's all going to turn out all right."

Book of Common Prayer 1979
Lord God Almighty, maintain our liberties in righteousness and peace.

A Prayer of Forgiveness—Donna L.K. Chiacchia
Heavenly Father, I come before you today to ask Your forgiveness and to seek your direction and guidance.
I know Your Word says, 'Woe to those who call evil good,' but that is exactly what I have done.
I have lost my spiritual equilibrium.
I have ridiculed the time-honored values of our forefathers and believe it to be enlightenment.
Search me, Oh, God, and know my heart today; cleanse me from every sin and set me free. Amen!

Great Women, Great Quotes

Edith Stein, St. Teresa Benedicta of the Cross
"Let go of your plans. The first hour of your morning belongs to God. Tackle the day's work that He charges you with, and He will give you the power to accomplish it.

Eleanor Roosevelt
"No one can make you feel inferior without your consent."

Carol Burnett
"Only I can change my life. No one can do it for me."

Erma Bombeck
"It takes courage to show your dreams to someone else."

Ann Landers
"The true measure of an individual is how he treats a person who can do him absolutely no good."

Erica Jong
"Advice is what we ask for when we already know the answer but wish we didn't."

Anne Frank
"Think of all the beauty still left around you and be happy."

SHE IS A SUNFLOWER! SHE BRINGS HOPE TO PEOPLE.—AVIJEET DAS

Mary Pickford

"If you have made mistakes, even serious ones, there is always another chance for you. What we call failure is not the falling down, but the staying down."

Alice Paul

"When you put your hand to the plow, you can't put it down until you get to the end of the row."

Noela Evans

"Challenge is a dragon with a gift in its mouth... Tame the dragon and the gift is yours."

Helen Keller

"Always be a first-rate version of yourself instead of a second-rate version of someone else."

Eleanor Roosevelt

"I gain strength, courage and confidence by every experience in which I must stop and look fear in the face...I say to myself, I've lived through this and can take the next thing that comes along."

Judy Garland
"When one door of happiness closes, another opens; but often we look so long at the closed door that we do not see the one which has opened for us."

Renita Weems
"I cannot forget my mother. She is my bridge.
When Ineeded to get across, she steadied herself
long enough for me to run across safely."

Rose Kennedy
"I have come to the conclusion that the most important element in human
life is faith. If God were to take away all blessings, health, physical fitness,
wealth, intelligence and leave but one gift, I would ask for faith — for with
faith in God, in God's goodness, mercy, love for me, and belief in ever
lasting life, I believe I could still be happy, trustful, leaving all to God's
inscrutable providence."

Coco Chanel
"How many cares one loses when one decides not to be something but to be someone."

Shirley Chisholm
"Service is the rent you pay for room on this planet."

Mary Anne Radmacher
Courage" does not always roar, sometimes, it is the quiet voice at the end of the day saying "I will try again tomorrow."

Katharine Butler Hathaway
"There is nothing better than the encouragement of a good friend."

Martha Stewart
"Life is too complicated not to be orderly."

Pioneer Girls Leaders' Handbook
"A friend hears the song in my heart and sings it to me when my memory fails."

Gloria Steinem
"We have become the men we wanted to marry."

Of Presidents and Great Men

Thomas Jefferson
"Nothing gives one person so much advantage over another as to remain always cool and unruffled under all circumstances."

TOMORROW MAY RAIN, SO I'LL
FOLLOW THE SUN.—THE BEATLES

Abraham Lincoln
"Determine that the thing can and shall be done, and then we shall find the way."

"What kills a skunk is the publicity it gives itself."

"Whatever you are, be a good one."

"All I am or hope to be I owe to my angel mother."

John F. Kennedy
"When written in Chinese, the word "crisis" is composed of two characters—one represents danger, and the other represents opportunity."

"Conformity is the jailer of freedom and the enemy of growth."

Jimmy Carter
"We should live our lives as though Christ was coming this afternoon."

Ronald Reagan
"Politics is supposed to be the second oldest profession. I have come to realize that it bears a very close resemblance to the first."

George W. Bush
"The peaceful transfer of authority is rare in history, yet common in our country. With a simple oath, we affirm old traditions and make new beginnings."

Abraham Lincoln
"You have to do your own growing no matter how tall your grandfather was."

Thomas A. Edison
"Opportunity is missed by most people because it is dressed in overalls and looks like work."

Benjamin Franklin
"God governs in the affairs of men. And if a sparrow cannot fall to the ground without His notice, is it probable then an empire can rise without His aid?"

Albert Pike
"What we have done for ourselves alone dies with us; what we have done for others and the world remains and is immortal."

Mahatma Gandhi
"When I despair, I remember that all through history the way of truth and love has always won. There have been tyrants, and murderers, and for a time they can seem invincible, but in the end they always fall, always."

"A coward is incapable of exhibiting love; it is the prerogative of the brave."

H. Jackson Brown, Jr.
"Live so that when your children think of fairness, caring and integrity, they think of you."

Ralph Waldo Emerson
"Do not go where the path may lead, go instead where there is no path and leave a trail."

Oliver Wendell Holmes, Jr.
"Man's mind, once stretched by a new idea, never regains its original dimensions."

Francois Muriac
"No love, no friendship can cross the path of our destiny without leaving some mark on it forever."

Andre Gide
"There are very few monsters that warrant the fear we have of them."

Charles Kingsley
"We act as though comfort and luxury were the chief requirements of life, when all that we need to make us really happy is something to be enthusiastic about."

Nicholas Murray Butler
"Optimism is essential to achievement and it is also the foundation of courage and of true progress."

Coleman Cox
"I am a great believer in luck. The harder I work the more of it I seem to have."

Alphonse Karr
"Every man has three characters: that which he shows, that which he has, and that which he thinks he has."

THE MORNING GLORIES AND THE SUNFLOWERS TURN NATURALLY TOWARD THE LIGHT, BUT WE HAVE TO BE TAUGHT, IT SEEMS.—RICHARD ROHR

Vincent Van Gogh
"The fishermen know that the sea is dangerous and the storm is terrible, but they have never found these dangers sufficient reason to remain ashore."

Mark Twain
"On with the dance; let joy be unconfined is my motto, whether there's any dance to dance or any joy to unconfined."

General George S. Patton
"Never tell people how to do things. Tell them what to do and they will surprise you with their ingenuity."

Family Affair

...remember you have me and I've got you.

LEGEND AND LEGACY:
MY MOTHER, JOYCE

The words legend and legacy have been used quite a bit since February 3rd and February 4th of 2022. Legend has been used when discussing my dad, and legacy, well, that word has been focused upon me. I beg to differ with those using those words to describe anyone other than my mother, Joyce Mowry.

She was and is my constant inspiration. I defined her in a simple list of seven items that I told myself to remember, every day, to be: Organized, disciplined, analytical, focused, creative, realistic, and compassionate. All the things Joyce required to create the heaven on earth in which I lived. It is what my mother-in-law calls, "a charmed life". I didn't realize what she meant until the true "charm" of my life left me in a shroud of wonder.

Joyce was so many things to so many people but the role she took most seriously was being my mother. She was the mother that everyone dreamed of having…and there were many of my close friends that asked if they could be "adopted". This is certainly not to diminish anyone else's mom; it is simply how sublimely engaging she was in her own quiet way. She was, quite simply, a truly lovely woman. She saw everyone as they wanted to be, versus who they presented themselves to be. You were immediately elevated, in her eyes, to your best self.

My Mother's legacy will live on in the legendary love she provided for those she cared for professionally and personally. There is none greater.

THANK YOU, MOM.

This is to honor my first mentor in the "business" of life. I wrote this a few decades ago and while we were going through some files together, we reminisced...

I LOVE YOU, DAD.

A BIRTHDAY MESSAGE
TO MY FATHER, LEON

I am so grateful that I have a true visionary and genius for a father.

Thank-you so much for being with me and giving me the opportunity to be on the ground floor of greatness.

I pray that we will always have respect and love for each other this day and every day.

I pray that when the opportunities come our way, we will stay humble and thankful, never squandering the fortune we achieve.

My greatest gift and fortune are that I have you for a father. I hope you have many more years to spend with me.

HAPPY BIRTHDAY.
YOUR DAUGHTER, YUMMIE

*Dad spent several more years with me
until his passing on February 3, 2022.
Rest in Peace and Rise in Glory dear Father.*

To My Beloved Sister-In-Law

It seems that every thought I have is a silent prayer to God, and at times vocalized even if I'm all by myself. Without the knowledge of having the Lord God as my constant companion, I'm sure I'd be nowhere in my life.

As a result, I wanted to share with you something I came across. Several years ago, a journalist by the name of John Stossel (he's part of the 20/20 news group) did a piece entitled **"Happiness—Who Has It and How to Get It"**.

I was very impressed with this piece. I remembered it and ordered the manuscript because I couldn't locate the piece of paper I took notes on about the piece from 1997.

In any event, here are the four alleged ingredients for happiness according to many renowned psychologists, psychiatrists, and philosophers. I'm also (how could I not) adding some of my own commentary on these items. I thought the four items made sense but I needed to take it up a notch.

The first item is CONTROL.

I took issue with this. I don't believe we have control. God has all the control, what we have is free will. This free will is bestowed upon us by God. We are born with it and are either tormented by it or mange it to our advantage. The effective management of that free will through any given circumstance or situation enables us to have some measure of control but we ultimately, whether we want to or not, being one of God's children, give all the control to Him. Many times this is learned the hard way. In other words, Stuff Happens while we're making other plans!

I figure if I can manage—at an even keel—this free will, I'll be doing pretty well. A good example of this "control versus free will" thing is illustrated in the Bible, the book of Job.

The second item is OPTIMISM.

It seems according to the psychologists, psychiatrists, and philosophers we are all born with a certain amount of optimism. To many of us the glass is always half-full and to others, the glass is always half-empty. I believe that optimism may be learned as well as bred.

My mother told me that when I was born, 6 weeks premature, 4lbs and 3 oz., I was pretty grouchy and did not, under any circumstances, want to be touched unless I cried for food or changing. Evidently I wasn't born with a "work and play well with others" attitude.

I was checked out thoroughly and it was determined I was just tiny and grouchy but nothing was medically wrong with me. My mom set out to train me how to accept interaction with others and by the time I got to nursery school I was pretty much the most gregarious, friendly little shaver you ever wanted to meet.

Moving forward to the present, I can't imagine wasting my time with the doom and gloom dance and always try to find some good in a situation no matter how heinous and impossible it may seem at the time. Once I lose my focus on staying optimistic and develop an attitude problem, one of the four items to being happy, is jeopardized and it really just makes mefeel bad.

So, the moral of this item is, as you have said in the past: "Nothing matters and everything matters". I just keep my little head down and try to plow forward with a smile on my face.

The third item is MEANINGFUL ACTIVITY.

Now here is an item I so agree with, that I would have put it first. Do I need to say anymore on this one? You have seen me in action. I am generally a proactive high energy kind of gal. This does put some people off but guess what....tough!

You know my motto—The only opinion of yourself that matters is your own. Do what is in your heart. Try not to break a Ten Commandment or a federal law and I think everything is going to be OK. Serve others and you have served our Lord.

I love it when I've latched on to something and every morning I can't wait to do it, whatever it is, professional or personal. We may as well do something meaningful while we are here; it is, after all, a very short time.

The last item is CLOSE RELATIONSHIPS.

I could really go on about this one but I will simply say this: The first close relationship I want and need is to God. The second close relationship I want and need is to myself. After that, it's all gravy as far as I'm concerned.

We come in alone, we go out alone. And yet, we are never alone because we always have our Lord by our side.

He loves to go everywhere with us; in fact He wants us to take Him. Further, whether we remember to bring Him along or not, it's funny how He always shows up when we really need Him. Now that's what I call a close relationship.

I love you. Always remember that. Take care. Donna

EVERY FLOWER
BLOOMS AT A
DIFFERENT PACE.
—SUZY KASSEM

**Left to right, sister-in-law Billi-Jo, my brother Jason, and I having a family dinner together.
Credit: Author**

A POEM TO MY HUSBAND TOM

Sleep well my love, do not despair.

We will make it through no matter where

we must go or what we must do;

remember you have me and I've got you.

WHO KNOWS WHAT MAY LIE AROUND THE NEXT CORNER? THERE MAY BE A WINDOW SOMEWHERE AHEAD. IT MAY LOOK OUT ON A FIELD OF SUNFLOWERS.—JOE HILL

A Short Story About Painting

Bob Merrill, Lyricist
"Don't tell me not to fly, I've simply got to—"

Donna and Debbie

When we were growing up, all of us wanted to be one of the cool kids. All of us were interested in being popular. All of us wanted to be the center of attention, at least for 15 minutes.

Well, the fact is, my cousin Debbie was, at least in my eyes, THE cool kid. I wanted to be pretty and cute and blonde, just like her. She was always the center of my attention.

When she was born, she was my special baby doll. Of course my Godmother and mother needed to monitor my inter-action. Usually, I couldn't get that good a hold of Debbie so I would just pick her up by the neck and then eventually I could get those long legs and the rest of her positioned into my arms so I could carry her everywhere.

Of course, I was only two years old so the carrying wasn't a long experience but certainly long enough for her mother and my mother to put up with, and, just enough for our grandmother to rescue her grandchildren, one from the other.

Need I say more? We were inseparable. It was by the sheer determination of my Godmother that Debbie was not chocked, dropped, suffocated or squeezed to death before the age of two.

Once Debbie got big enough, I decided to get down to business...Barbie doll business.

THE
SUNFLOWER
IS A FAVORITE
EMBLEM OF
CONSTANCY.
—THOMAS
BULFINCH

The Barbie doll world we created had a definite system. Donna and Debbie were in charge of setting things up and maneuvering Barbie. My cousin Susan was in charge of not messing anything up and cousin Donald was in charge of swallowing no less than 2 pairs of Barbie doll shoes.

The assemblage of adults, not allowed in Barbie world, were in charge of drinking as many cups of coffee as it would take for Donna and Debbie to be satisfied that we had played enough Barbie.

Let me clue you in, there isn't that much coffee in the world, not even in Columbia.

After we got tired of testing the adults over Barbie we moved to young adulthood and really gave them a run for their money.

Now, I definitely wanted to be Debbie. She had the legs, the blonde hair, the best sense of humor; she was after all, the most popular kid around and I thought she was so cool.

Debbie, from a young age was a gifted artist. I could barely manage to draw a stick figure. She was so deep, exotic and intense. I was always mesmerized at the way she could command the attention of anyone with her wit and style. She was so elegant.

Even though I was the oldest, she probably never knew that I always felt as though I walked in her shadow. I did not mind, I just wanted to be with Debbie.

WHEREVER LIFE PLANTS YOU, BLOOM WITH GRACE.
—OLD FRENCH PROVERB

37

Finally, Debbie gave me the chance to distinguish myself in her life. I would get to do something for a cool kid, I might even get to hang out with some other cool kids; you know, really be part of the gang.

Debbie asked me to choreograph a dance for her, for the Miss Teen USA Pageant. This was a big deal. I was so excited to finally be of some use to my cousin.

She brought down the house with her routine and I was so excited and proud. Debbie could do it all; she had brains, talent, style and best of all she was MY cousin. The music she chose will resonate forever in my mind; "Don't Rain on My Parade", from the musical "Funny Girl".

It simply sums up what Deborah believed her life would be. Here is an excerpt from the immortal lyricist, Bob Merrill:

> *"If you live your life, life is bound to teach you,*
> *that you're half alive unless you let life reach you."*

> *"I've been a machine, push a button and*
> *I dance, turn a handle and I sing."*

> *"Now this machine is going to fly and just one guy*
> *will wind the spring."*

> *"Don't tell me not to fly, I've simply got to—*
> *if someone takes a spill it's me and not you,*
> *don't bring a cloud around to rain on my parade."*

Deborah, your fidelity to your hopes and dreams has cleared away every cloud in your path.

Your sky is blue and clear and now you have all eternity to paint and create on a canvas that covers this universe.

I will watch for your brush strokes in the clouds, your message to everyone on earth that loves you.

In Memory of my beautiful and beloved Cousin,
Deborah Ann Voelker Bergeron

There's More To It...

I knew she had come to say good-bye.

The Rest of Shirley's Story

Today is a day for celebration. Perhaps this sounds unusual, or perhaps to some, even disrespectful but I know, to my Godmother, Shirley, this coming from her Goddaughter would not be anything like that. She was uniquely a person that "got it." She knew exactly what was going on and going down.

I was asked by her daughter, my cousin Susan and her son, my cousin Donald, to deliver her tribute and please know that it is with the greatest humility and respect that I speak today on my Godmother's behalf; besides which, her parents, my grandparents, Raymond and Violette Mowry, are here with me now on my right and left and so we know it will be our best work. I was prompted to entitle this tribute, "The Rest of the Story", because of the riveting and descriptive (not) obituary in the Woonsocket Call.

While it is true that my Auntie was a homemaker, this doesn't quite tell the rest of the story, so I beg some indulgence as I portray Shirley Ann Mowry Voelker from the eyes of those closest to her. Shirley was a beautiful girl and woman. She was, in fact, considered by many to be dazzling in the "looks" department and possessed a pair of legs rivaled only by the famous Betty Grable.

She was vivacious, witty and had a wonderful sense of humor. She mastered the art of the "one liner" from her mother. Right up until a day before her passing she remarked about some conversation with one of her more colorful and favorite expressions, her bright blue eyes twinkling and a small smile curling up around her mouth.

Shirley's ability to make everyone feel at home and welcomed was one of her best assets evidenced by the fact that her home was always the place everyone wanted to frequent for playtime, mealtime, anytime.

We just liked being at Aunt Shirley's house. Best food, best games and of course my cousins were there to play with and or torture. So, the homemaker thing is a fair description but not the whole picture. Shirley was a strong, resourceful person. She had lots of street savvy and was a veracious reader. She quickly became a favored employee wherever she took up part-time work. Her personality and horse sense endeared her to everyone and her ability to understand the business part of what she was doing was uncanny. No MBA necessary for Shirley, she just "got it!"

She always loved to cook and was a wonderful gourmet. She was a co-owner of a restaurant on Main Street in Woonsocket for several years and the food was some of the best the city had to offer.

Folks would put their orders in advance to be sure they got the "special" of the day before it was sold out. The reason I know this is that I got turned away a couple of times so

...A SATELLITE DISH FOR SUNSHINE.
—HELEN MIRREN

I learned to call in my order from the road when I was consulting so that I wouldn't miss out on some of my favorite dishes.

So, now we have another piece of the puzzle, Shirley the chef/business person but, the best pieces of this whole picture are yet to come.

She defended those she cared for, even when our behavior did not merit such. She gave this love and loyalty unconditionally and only demanded in return a little respect and good behavior on our part, which most of the time we accomplished.

Shirley's ability to give seemed endless. No matter how limited her resources, she managed to always find something to give for every situation. Her presentation was always so special. No matter what it was you were receiving from Shirley, it always felt like the most grand thing and make no mistake, it certainly was once you caught on to what she was actually giving.

Shirley, the private at-home person, was a wonderful sister and friend. Her sister Joyce was genuinely one of her favorite people and she considered her sister to be her best friend.

Mom, if you were not aware of that, now you are...
she told me this herself.

Shirley's character excelled when it came to love and loyalty. She loved her children (that includes me—I was her fourth child) and gave with all her heart to the very best of her ability. She simply adored her grandchildren and came to know her great-grandchildren in her final days.

This love and loyalty that was bestowed upon us was the greatest treasure.

So now, we have the cornerstone pieces of the puzzle but the picture would not be complete without this last piece, illustrated by this story. Right up until her last moments on earth, she was giving; Here's the story:

January 9th is a big date in my life. It is the date that I accepted work as a consultant which materially changed my life and more especially it is the date that my husband asked me to marry him. Those events have now been eclipsed by Shirley, the greatest of givers.

The evening of January 9th, Aunt Shirley came to me while I was sleeping rather restlessly, fretting over something or another. I knew she had come to say good-bye the moment I heard the whisper of her voice and felt her touch. She held me for a while and stroked my hair and told me not to fret over anything, that all would be fine.

And then, she was gone, a gentle fragrant mist passing before me. She gave her last gift to me that night, her reassurance that there is eternal life and that she has gone on in peace.

Now you have the rest of the story...
Go forward and celebrate Shirley's life!

It's Just Business

"We may as well try."
We did try…she succeeded…
so did the project.

Need hope?

Five Attributes of Leading From Behind To Disrupt the Status Quo

► Set your "consultant-cap" aside and set others up for SUCCESS.

► Set clear goals, guidelines and EXPECTATIONS.

► EMPOWER your client, remove obstacles in their path, challenge them.

► Give frequent feedback: TRUST but verify.

► Cut them loose! ALLOW them to own the successes that follow.

HOW WILL YOUR CLIENT FEEL ABOUT THIS TECHNIQUE?

Protected: "I do not even know they are here, but I can feel their presence."

Empowered: "It is like I have this invisible secret weapon."

Secure: "But when we need them, they are there."

"WE ARE HEARD...UNDERSTOOD...VALUED. WE TRUST THEM."

BASED UPON THE TEACHINGS OF LAO TZU

**"When the best leader's work is done—
the people say, 'we did it ourselves.'"**

COSMETIC TIPS

Getting It Right Takes FOCUS

Can COSMETIC tips play a significant role in Project LEADERSHIP?

Our client, a mid-level manager with a Fortune 500 insurance carrier, worked diligently on perfecting a key performance report for senior management. We had spent a week to ensure that every significant productivity and utilization factor was recorded and translated for easy consumption by the executive level.

The manager and I had built a good working relationship. We were on the same page about the intention and scope of what was expected. I came to realize in this final session, prior to the report being presented, just how "good", good was.

The finishing touches were being dealt with as we sat closely, going over the report. Finally, we had it just as we wanted. I sat back, turned to her, and asked her, "Do you have any other questions?"

She replied, "Yes, I do. How do you get your eye liner on the bottom rim of your eye so neat? I can never make that happen."

I replied, "with the same level of focus as you have perfected this report."

Discipline and compassion created the report and the relationship.

The unique value we create together will be more than cosmetic.

KEEP YOUR FACE TO THE SUNSHINE AND YOU CANNOT SEE THE SHADOW. IT'S WHAT SUNFLOWERS DO.—HELEN KELLER

A New
FRESH
Set of Eyes
May Be
The Way

She said:

"We had 3 other people try to get this project on track and one of them was from a BIG FOUR firm… What makes you think you can fix this?"

So I said:

"We cannot fix this…. and you called us…." I am thinking to myself:

"DANGER!

Get out of this interview as quickly as you can. FAILURE ahead!"

54

But this exec was very DOWN…
maybe I would let her vent and then move on…
OR maybe there was an opportunity here…

She continued: "Yeah, I know YOU can't fix this…it's ME,
I must fix this. I apologize. My behavior is way off, but
I am in a jam."

I ENCOURAGED her: "Tell me what happened.
From the beginning. There may be a way. A NEW fresh set of eyes.
We may as well discuss it and if we cannot come up with an idea,
then we will let this die a dignified death, but leave you whole.
Deal?"

*She took a breath in and then…a litany that lasted for 20 minutes…
the three pre-crisis indicators had snuck up on her until she felt like
there was no turning back.*

1. **Restate the INTENTION of the project.**
2. **Harness the SCOPE back into budget.**
3. **Get the STAKEHOLDERS to buy back in.**

Still defeated, she listened and then agreed.
"WE MAY AS WELL TRY."

*We did try…she succeeded…
so did the project.*
Need hope?

A Funny Story
About a Lake,
a LinkedIn Coach,
and a Stripper...

I prepared a testimonial for my LinkedIn coach. It's used on the Master Class page, as well as his profile page.

Talk about great exposure!

I looked at the playback and thought, "wow, well isn't that a great shot of the burlesque advertisement in the background."

He asked if this was one of my hobbies, collecting vintage stripper posters. I said no. It was a gift from my brother-in-law. We have a lake house, and he thought it would be fun.

But I did share the story of how dazzled I was with the movie Gypsy Rose Lee. I was 12 years old and very into the performing arts. Trust me, 12 years old then, not the same as now.

I thought I wanted to be a stripper like Natalie Wood portraying Gypsy Rose Lee. My mother told me I was running around the house in my slip pretending to be her.

My mother didn't want to quash my enthusiasm for dancing but explained this type came with some stipulations, such as having relations with strange men.

I was horrified and immediately put my dress back on. That was the last of "stripping" ever discussed until one day, my client said to me, "could you just strip it down and keep it simple."

Turns out I'm a stripper after all! Boom chink!

7

Seven Compelling Traits That Are Key to Client Success

THE ROAD TO FREEDOM IS BORDERED WITH SUNFLOWERS.—MARTIN FIRRELL

1. Accountability

You hold yourself accountable. The buck stops with YOU and your actions always match your words.

2. Authenticity

You are authentically appreciative of others. Words truly matter and you always use them to communicate you care.

3. Optimism

You always find the silver lining. Your advantage mindset prevents you from being frustrated by negativity.

4. Instinct

You know when to move on and forward. You give things a G.U.T. check. Is it good, useful, true? If it does not check out, onward and upward!

5. Acceptance

You do not need to keep score. This activity is unnecessary in a world of abundance. There is plenty for everyone.

6. Curiosity

You are genuinely curious. The world is a wondrous place to you, filled with opportunity to thrive.

7. Aspiration

You strive for continuous improvement. You embrace the cracks of imperfection and the power of the light streaming through them.

What if I told you that INVESTING in these 3 things would IMPROVE your professional and personal life?

HOW?

It requires an ancient wisdom assessment used by Socrates...

1. IS IT A GOOD THING?
2. IS IT USEFUL?
3. IS IT TRUTHFUL?

It is easy to get sidetracked with a "shiny object".
We are human and we unwittingly succumb to drama and hearsay. We focus on habits that have zero to do with what is true for us, good for us, and useful for those around us. That is why we need an "advantage" mind-set.

Here is an example of how this works:
I was presented with an initiative to complete in a tight time frame which I expediently put through the "test".
I had conditioned myself to run the request through the automatic filter, set in my mind.

The "advantage" mind-set quickly assessed that:
▶ The client's employees (a.k.a. Brand Ambassadors) would benefit tangibly and intangibly—**GOOD**
▶ Their own clients would receive value, ensuring repeat sales—**USEFUL**
▶ They had been completely realistic about outcomes—**TRUTH**

ACQUIRING the "advantage mind-set" has CHANGED in the past 2000 years, its PRINCIPALS have not. The same formula that worked for Socrates then WORKS now.

Ready to invest in GOOD, USEFUL TRUTHS?

Good Advice

When you think the world
has turned its back on you,
take a look: you most likely
turned your back on the world.

I CAN'T FEEL BAD ABOUT BEING WHO I AM,
JUST LIKE THE GIRL NEXT TO ME CAN'T FEEL
BAD ABOUT BEING WHO SHE IS. "BECAUSE
A ROSE CAN NEVER BE A SUNFLOWER,
AND A SUNFLOWER CAN NEVER BE A ROSE.
—MIRANDA KERR

Facts of Life:

1. At least 2 people in this world love you so much they would die for you.
2. At least 15 people in this world love you in some way.
3. The only reason anyone would ever hate you is because they want to be just like you—or they are afraid that they are just like you.
4. A smile from you can bring happiness to anyone, even if they don't like you.
5. Every night, SOMEONE thinks about you before they go to sleep.
6. You mean the world to someone.
7. If not for you, someone may not be living.
8. You are special and unique.
9. Someone that you don't even know exists loves you.
10. When you make the biggest mistake ever, something good comes from it.
11. When you think the world has turned its back on you, take a look: you most likely turned your back on the world.
12. When you think you have no chance of getting what you want, you probably won't get it, but if you believe in yourself, probably, sooner or later, you will get it.
13. Always remember the compliments you received. Forget about the rude remarks.
14. Always tell someone how you feel about them; you will feel much better when they know.
15. If you have a great friend, take the time to let them know that they are great.

**Hold dear to your parents for it is a scary
and confusing world without them."**
EMILY DICKINSON

My parents, Joyce Mowry, right, and Leon Kayarian—Christmas 2013.
Credit: Author

My last words of wisdom:

**"Go to college and get the best
degree you can afford."**

I CHOSE A SUNFLOWER BECAUSE WHEN
DARKNESS DESCENDS THEY CLOSE UP
TO REGENERATE. —HALLE BERRY

God Wanted Me To Tell You

"It shall be well with you this year. No matter how much your enemies try this year, they will not succeed. You have been destined to make it and you shall surely achieve all your goals this year. For the remaining months of the year; all your agonies will be diverted and victory and prosperity will be incoming in abundance. Today God has confirmed the end of your sufferings, sorrows and pains because He that sits on the throne has remembered you. He has taken away the hardships and given you JOY. He will never let you down.

I knocked at heaven's door this morning. God asked me...

My child! What can I do for you?

And I said, Father, please protect and bless the person reading this message.

God smiled and answered...

"Request granted."

Wish I Had Said That!

Bob Moawad
"Creativity is God's gift to you.
What you do with it is your gift to God."

J. Askenberg
"You win some, you lose some, and some get rained out, but you gotta suit up for them all."

Somerset Maugham
"Perfection has one grave defect; it is apt to be dull."

William Law
"Pray, and let God worry."

Sigmund Freud
"One day in retrospect, the years of struggle will strike you as the most beautiful."

ITALIAN PROVERB
"Once the game is over, the king and the pawn go back into the same box."

ATTICUS THE POET

**I begged the universe for you and
one day you arrived as everything
I'd always asked for and it didn't
take me long to realize—
I should have been more specific.**

Bernard Edinger
"Inside the will of God there is no failure. Outside the will
of God there is no success."

Francois Muriac
"No love, no friendship can cross the path of our destiny."

Emanuel Swedenborg
"Conscience is God's presence in man."

Henry David Thoreau, "Inspiration"
"Whatever we leave to God, God does and blesses us."

Izaak Walton
"God has two dwellings; one in heaven, and the other in
a meek and thankful heart."

Charles C. West
"We turn to God for help when our foundations are shaking,
only to learn that it is God who is shaking them."

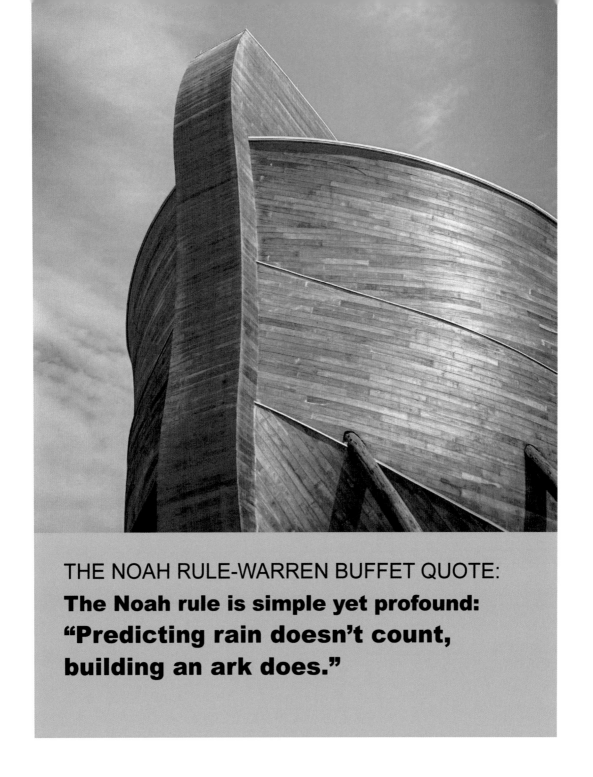

THE NOAH RULE-WARREN BUFFET QUOTE:

The Noah rule is simple yet profound: "Predicting rain doesn't count, building an ark does."

Chinese Epigram

If you are patient in one moment of anger, you will escape a hundred days of sorrow.

Henry Chester

"Enthusiasm is the greatest asset in the world. It beats money and power and influence."

J.P. de Caussade
"Since God offers to manage our affairs for us, let us once and for all hand them over to His infinite wisdom, in order to occupy ourselves only with Himself and what belongs to Him."

Charlotte Clemensen Taylor
"Coincidence is God's way of remaining anonymous."

Oscar Wilde
"People may fail many times, but they become failures only when they begin to blame someone else."

Steven Wright
"You cannot have everything. I mean, where would you put it?"

Andre Gide
"There are very few monsters that warrant the fear we have of them."

Josh Billings
"Be like a postage stamp. Stick to one thing until you get there."

A FLOWER DOES NOT USE WORDS TO ANNOUNCE
ITS ARRIVAL TO THE WORLD; IT JUST BLOOMS.
—MATSHONA DHLIWAYO

Supreme
Messages

Dive into all that is free and clear.

A LONG TIME AGO IN A KINGDOM BY THE SEA
THERE LIVED A PRINCESS AS TALL AND BRIGHT
AS A SUNFLOWER.—JEANNE DESY

Thank-You God For Blessing Me Much More Than I Deserve.

Being the underdog has a way of working out.
What year was this? 1963.
She did not realize, several decades later, her background would be considered commonplace.
This poor kid was homely and scrawny, an only child, being raised by a single parent.
Every day was endless boredom, learning to play games by herself. She would craft people to play with by cutting pictures out of a magazine and taping them to her bedpost.
Few playmates at school; the other kids were "warned" about her; she had divorced parents.
She was of middle eastern decent so in a small WASP town of less than 3K, this made her "black".
She tried to engage with the other kids but ended up taunted and bullied.
She would retreat into a corner somewhere in the play yard.
School was torture, home was lonely, but at least safe. Her only escape was dance and music.
She was comforted by Barbie and her kitties.
Her dance teacher, grandparents, mother, and dad—when he came to visit—were her playmates.
Even church was tough. No one would associate with her, she was an "unfortunate"; divorced parents.
Several decades past 1963, she transformed into a contender, a lighthouse to her clients.

Acknowledged. Understood. Accepted.

NEAL A. MAXWELL
**Each Of Us
Is An Innkeeper
Who Decides If There
Is Room For Jesus.**

GUILLAUME APOLLINAIRE

"Come to the edge."
"We can't. We're afraid."
"Come to the edge."
"We can't. We will fall!"
"Come to the edge."
  And they came.
  And he pushed them.
  And they flew.

What I have in this moment, is because I "made room" for it. Thank-you God for blessing me much more than I deserve. Happy Holidays to all my LinkedIn Community.
There is always room for YOU in my inn. —*DLKC*

78

Are you with me?

We are being given a "sign".
To dispense with our old ways and understand a new order is upon us.
A virus has blanketed the earth. It forced us into different patterns of work, economics, recreation, basic communication.
Imagine…a new approach.
Motivating ourselves for organization, discipline, focus, creativity, realism, and compassion.
Eliminating the spend on fear, panic, apathy, intellectual death.
Dive into all that is free and clear.
What do we have that is free and clear?
We have free will; free will to manage our lives in the most effective manner we are able.
Make a command decision to take control and manage your free will.
Then the way you "feel" will allow you towards a new and better way.
You got this.
There are 12 unique emotional scale feelings for a new and better way.
Enthusiasm, Eagerness, Happiness, Passion, Appreciation, Love, Freedom, Empowerment, Knowledge, Joy, Excellence, and Self-Transcendence.

Which of these will you embrace to follow YOUR star?

The Great Pilgrimage:

Theory One and Theory Two

The answer was easy.

Theory One: Whoever Pays Is In Charge

This theory was developed as I was driving to Casita on July 16, 2004. I reminisced about the way every one of the teens processed and executed a passionate request that I made regarding my husband.

My husband had gone to bed at about 8:30 PM that evening as he awakes at about 4:30 most days to go to work. I implored them, as they were coming off the roof of our condo from swimming, not to waken him and explained why this was so important.

They respectfully and very quietly tip toed into the condo, retrieved their things and tip toed back out without a sound. Some even had to enter the bedroom itself and they were so quiet that my husband was none the wiser and his precious sleep was not disturbed.

The next day as I was driving to Casita, it dawned on me how maturely the teens had processed this request. It also occurred to me that my husband is mostly handling everything financially at this time, and he's doing all the "paying" so I can afford to run around Puerto Rico for 10 days with these teenagers. As a result, when he asks pretty much anything of me, I believe it is his marital privilege that I go along with his requests; in other words, I do, at some level, "obey" him.

This idea was then extended to the very core of my existence and I asked myself who has "paid" the highest price ever for me. The answer was easy. Jesus Christ paid with His life for me, that I may know Him in eternity which is where, as a Christian, I believe I am headed.

Further, if I am true to my Christian faith, then it would be logical that if Jesus has done all the "paying" then I am obligated to "obey" Him and only Him.

Bottom line:
Jesus Christ is in charge—
He has done all the paying.

Theory Two: God's Will Always Prevails

This theory is actually more fact than theory. Free will is one of my favorite topics. I decided to create a theory about free will in order to create a discussion forum for the Pilgrims as we drove around Puerto Rico. These discussions proved to alleviate a bit of the challenging driving conditions we came across on a daily basis.

We are given free will by God. It is His gift to us at our birth. This means we are able to think and do anything we want, as long as we are also willing to accept whatever consequences and results are associated with our actions.

This does not, however, make you in charge. As illustrated in theory one, Jesus Christ (God the Son) is in charge.

Now that you are a young adult, we begin to look at free will from a different perspective.

We are not given free will to make us in charge, think and do anything we want, and then God will bring up the rear and clean it all up for us like we are children.

We are given free will to do those things which benefit ourselves, those around us, and to glorify God, whom without, we would have nothing.

God does not mess around with our free will. He doesn't need to because whatever you decide to do, He will in some way thwart if it does not fit into His overall Master Plan for the universe and you.

God's will ultimately prevails because He, and not us, is in charge of the final outcome. We are here to assist Him and do His will and He allows us the freedom to find our way and understand His way. This is why we are taught to pray and in silence and prayer we are able to hear God's will for us.

A true and actual manifestation of this theory was experienced by me on this Pilgrimage which is shared in the following excerpt from my journal.

Bottom line:
Control = The effective
management of free will.

THE FLOWER THAT FOLLOWS
THE SUN DOES SO EVEN
IN CLOUDY DAYS.
—ROBERT LEIGHTON

84

DONNA L. K. CHIACCHIA

We are given free will by God. It is His gift to us at our birth. This means we are able to think and do anything we want, as long as we are also willing to accept whatever consequences and results are associated with our actions.

Excerpt From My Pilgrimage Journal

Perhaps now that I get it, I'll catch a break.

Journal excerpt July 21, 2004

Father David led us in Morning Prayer that day and then asked us at about 9:30 A.M. if we would observe a time of complete silence until noon time. Everyone was allowed to explore the mountain retreat in groups of two. I went off on a few trails that took me through some coffee plantations and along the road going towards some other farming areas in the mountains. The vistas were actually some of the most beautiful I have ever seen and this time gave me a chance to hear God.

I had been skeptical about going into the mountains because I was afraid and also because we had gotten sidetracked a few too many times for my liking. I expressed my concerns to those pilgrims I had with me and they reassured me they were up for the challenge.

So off we went and everything turned out to be beautiful.

In the last 20 minutes of silence I entered the following into my journal:

My journey began when I met all of these wonderful teens; at first, I didn't care for them very much but then I found I cared for them more than I thought possible. I have taken them as of this point, mostly where I have always wanted to take them and now I see that most of them have so many gifts, they are ready to surpass even the dreams and hopes I have fantasized for them.

We discussed how we felt as adults. I told them my feelings —I didn't sugar coat—they have opened their hearts to me which I will never betray. Yes, it is true, they are adults. More polishing required but nonetheless, adults. And they will be something! They are ready!

Now I know why we have had all the mishaps; because they could not possibly learn anything if God did not put the adults in a position of making mistakes and then being forced to process these mistakes in front of those who must learn from us.

This is why —I wanted everything to be perfect and God wanted everything to be "adult-like" for them, which means sometimes, no matter what we try—God's will always prevails.

Perhaps now that I get it, I'll catch a break.

Glory to God in the highest and praise Him for giving me the opportunity through these young people to personally grow as well as provide them with information to soar past us.

It is always in that stillness that God can speak to you. If you ask, you will receive but you must be silent and open.

You must discipline yourself to be humble in His presence and have no fear that this humility is weakness. Indeed; it is strength. In cases of the extreme, it is pure heroic endurance.

God loves discipline and structure. Our free will is accentuated and tested when we are beholden to the great beauty He has created.

It creates a forum for us to demonstrate our love and praise for Him.

If we have heroic endurance for all the ups and downs of this life, then we are granted the great gift of the straight line and that line is called eternity.

Stay Cool

Life is a project. We live it one day at a time.

IN MY DNA:
Project: Barbie!

When I was growing up, I wanted to be one of the cool kids, at least for 15 minutes.

My cousin Debbie was, in my eyes, THE cool kid. She was the center of my attention. We were inseparable.

When she was born, she was my special baby doll that I would pick up (unfortunately, sometimes by one limb) and carry everywhere. Our grandmother would come to rescue her grandchildren, one from the other.

Once Debbie got big enough, I decided to get down to business. Barbie doll business.

The Barbie doll world we created had a definite system and my "project leadership" kicked into full gear. As it turns out, project leadership was in my DNA. I managed so set things up and Debbie maneuvered Barbie. My other two cousins were given charge of not messing up the plan. And being Project Leader WAS cool!

The adults, not allowed in Barbie world, were to drink as much coffee as it would take for Debbie and me to be satisfied we had played enough Barbie.

As it turned out, there is not that much coffee in the world. This was a long-term project, successfully completed 3 years later. I had achieved the ripe old age of 12 years and Debbie, 10 years.

We measured our success by passing down all the Barbie gear to our neighbors and staying a unified team to go on to the next "project".

Life is a project. We live it one day at a time.

I turned out pretty cool.

The State of Curious Calm

I am in a state of "CURIOUS CALM".

The State of Curious Calm is a space of freedom to explore whatever channel is required; spiritual, intellectual, physical.

You can freely enter this space. It's a space where free willl is honed and tested.

You will be faced with yourself, but you will not be alone.

WE'RE ALL GOLDEN SUNFLOWERS INSIDE.
—ALLEN GINSBERG

You will be with ALL your being. You will be able to explore your questions.

That's why the space is "curious calm"; I am curious to know how outside forces will attempt to infiltrate our free will.

I am curious to see how the effects of 2+ years of social distancing will affect our day-to-day decisions. The irony of "social distancing" is it brings people closer.

We are forced to sharpen our communication skills. We do not have to be F2F to build intellectual and emotional bonds. You're invited to this space. The space of curious calm.

Have you found your state of curious calm?

Cherry Tree Wisdom

PERFECTION IN PROGRESS is how I see the Cherry Tree.

It serves us being present in our lives and was a "present" to me for Easter 2020. There is a moment of reflection for the way each (present versus presence) has made me feel….How it being present in my life and…How the gift has transformed me over the past 7 weeks.

Being there, in the honor of its planting, created happiness for me; transformed me inwardly…to understand the tree's purpose in the history of our home and in the history of our time.

The Cherry Tree has taught me to share whatever gifts it has given me for the sake of building a life of service and being an instrument of its perfection in progress over the last 7 weeks.

We enter this world perfect according The Universe's unique gifts bestowed upon us, our free will.

Our progress may be assessed by not allowing ourselves to conform to the standards of this world but allowing our free will to inwardly change our minds.

Then we will be able to know the wisdom of our personal reflections; what is good and is pleasing to us as individuals, and is perfect in its presence, perfection in our own unique progress.

Acknowledge, Understand and then Accept

When anyone offers feedback on any topic it is from their perspective. It belongs to them. We have the free will to embrace it or not. Always be grateful and thankful for feedback. It is, after all, an acknowledgment that you exist, you are part of someone's radar.

WE MAY FIND OURSELVES TOO STEEPED IN THE "NOISE" OF EVERYONE'S FEEDBACK TO TRULY IDENTIFY THE RECURRING "SIGNAL" TO RESPOND TO...OUR OWN INNER SIGNAL.

Unless you can authentically be grateful and thankful for whatever feedback you receive, then you are, in fact, saying "thanks but no thanks". As a business owner you are continuously, and thankfully receiving feedback.

SUNFLOWERS END UP FACING THE SUN, BUT THEY GO THROUGH A LOT OF DIRT TO FIND THEIR WAY THERE.
— J.R. RIM

How would you otherwise know what your clients feel and think? How are we to succeed without being extremely mindful and respectful of their ownership of their feedback?

No matter what the feedback is, we are compelled to make a very deliberate decision on what to do with that information. Remember: "We may find ourselves too steeped in the "noise" of everyone's feedback to truly identify the recurring "signal" to respond to...our own inner signal.

WE BELIEVE THIS IS WHERE GROWTH HAPPENS, IN THE INNER SIGNAL WHICH OF COURSE COMES FROM RECURRING PATTERNS OF FEEDBACK.

The perspective of quieting ego and how that can be obtained through gratitude is another important viewpoint of acknowledging and accepting feedback. We must always be mindful and respectful of someone's feedback and their ownership of it. If we are cavalier in our response, then this could possibly be considered arrogant. That said, if we are very deliberate in determining what we will keep from the feedback, then we are winning at honing this all-important skill.

THE RESEARCH ON FEEDBACK IS CLEAR. THE FEEDBACK IS AT LEAST 50% FROM ANOTHER PERSON'S PERSPECTIVE. IT IS TRUE THAT COLLECTING MORE DATA POINTS *MAY* HIGHLIGHT A PATTERN BUT IT COULD ALSO SIMPLY VALIDATE THE EXISTING BIAS. *WHERE* AND *FROM WHOM* ONE COLLECTS THESE FEEDBACK "DATAPOINTS" IS AS CRITICAL AS THE FEEDBACK ITSELF.

The first thing is to de-stigmatize "feedback". We have lost the art of constructive and rational discourse. The idea of staying curious about all perspectives regarding one's performance can only be uplifting if the data is used appropriately. The simple approach is to acknowledge, understand, and then accept.

NO ONE SAID YOU AGREED. ACCEPTANCE IS NOT AGREEMENT. IN FACT, IT IS MUCH BETTER THAN AGREEMENT. IT LEVELS THE PLAYING FIELD SO THE DATA POINTS CAN DANCE WITH EASE.

An Aquired Taste?

That's A Compliment!

My clients have often defined my company's UNCOMMON value as an ACQUIRED taste.

They made clear
it was a compliment.

What does that "taste" like?
MY CLIENTS SAY IT TASTES LIKE…
- ▶ **FREEDOM** from "this doesn't work anymore"
- ▶ **ARRIVING** to their vision's happy place
- ▶ **LIVING** in a Circle of Psychological Safety and Trust

How do my clients "feel" once they have had a taste?
MY CLIENTS SAY THEY FEEL…
- ▶ **LIBERATED** from "this doesn't work anymore"
- ▶ **EMPOWERED** by realizing their vision successfully implemented
- ▶ **SECURE** in the Circle of Psychological Safety and Trust they created

Why do they feel this way?
My CLIENTS say they feel this way because they RECEIVED…
- ▶ Something **SPECIFIC** to their tastes.
- ▶ A **PERMANENT** vacation from "this doesn't work anymore."
- ▶ Passage on The Intentional Journey©™…the journey custom-designed **BY** them and **FOR** them.

This is my WHY.
It is JOYFUL to see clients…
- ▶ **THRIVE** in their own unique taste.
- ▶ **FEEL** liberated, empowered, secure.
- ▶ **RECEIVE** the permanent vacation they experience on their journey.

Who's ready for a vacation?

To those who have purchased this book...

This is seventeen years in the making...never got around to making it something "official". Official meaning, for "sale".

The years 2020 to 2023 were a rollercoaster of major events. A pandemic is a horrible thing. Losing both your parents in a 34-hour period is tough stuff.

That year (2020) forced me to do many things I had not done in a while, and I needed to do. The most important thing is it kept me from having to hang out with people I did not actually like. And people that did not understand me nor did they want to.

Surround yourself with people that "get" you and love you. Love is such a funny word.

Here's how I know someone "gets" me, likes me, or the grand slam "loves" me. I know they feel these things towards me when they look at me. I never have to chase after them. They are people who want to be with me and care about me. They are always present with me because of the way they make me feel when I am with them and then when I am not.

I want everyone to find people and circumstances like this in your life. Where there is love, freedom, empowerment, knowledge, and most of all JOY! These people and circumstances you will find for yourselves. No one can do it for you. If you're game, let's jump start the journey.

Together.

DON'T WAIT FOR SOMEONE
TO BRING YOU FLOWERS.
PLANT YOUR OWN GARDEN
AND DECORATE YOUR OWN
SOUL.– LUTHER BURBANK

STAY COOL

Much love and
peace to you and yours

*Siblings,
Luigi and
Lucille
Chiacchia
—June 2023
Credit: Author*

Printed in the United States
by Baker & Taylor Publisher Services